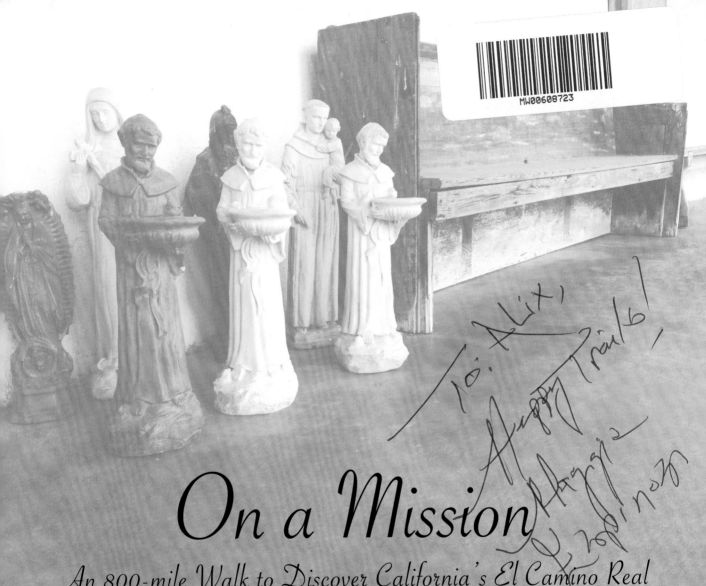

On a Mission

An 800-mile Walk to Discover California's El Camino Real

By **Maggie Espinosa**

Introduction

On November 15, 2013, I laced up my Nike Pegasus and embarked on a 800-mile walk to discover California's 21missions. I wasn't soul searching. I'm not an endurance athlete. I'm an ordinary 54-year old woman.

I divided my peregrination into 12 months, taking four days each month to cover approximately 75 miles, with Amtrak as my chauffeur to and fro. Google maps and Ron Briery's book, *A Hiker's Guide to California's 21 Spanish Missions Along El Camino Real*, were my compass. Prior to launch I sent an email inviting friends and family to join me on any segment of the excursion. A surprising number said yes.

My fellow pilgrims were from all walks of life, ages, professions, and religious beliefs – a flight attendant, a medical writer, an architect, a Franciscan Friar, a symphony bass player, a pet groomer, a teacher – all brought together by California's Royal Road. The southernmost mission, San Diego de Alcala, was the starting point. During the exhausting 20-plus-mile days, life stories were regaled, jaw-dropping sunsets witnessed and thousands of laughs shared. This was the blueprint each month.

Along the way my companions and I expected sore bodies and pep talks when fatigue commandeered our fervor. What we didn't expect was the kindness of strangers. The California Mission Walkers (CMW), a group of El Camino Real enthusiasts, followed my escapades on Facebook. Having never met any members, I was astonished when affiliates asked to walk with me, and with nothing more than an email to acquaint us, graciously provided guest rooms and meals to my cadre.

On November 5, 2014, I reached the final mission with my husband by my side. Tears streamed from my eyes as a year's worth of emotions surfaced. I'd accomplished a daunting goal: the 11th person to complete this sojourn. I learned such valuable lessons. Relationships are the heartbeat of life. There is a reserve deep inside everyone when called upon. Humanity is good.

Thank you to all my co-walkers for joining me on this experience of a lifetime. It would not have been the same without you.

The following pages are stories and photos I posted on Facebook during each segment of the walk. As the journey progressed, my entries became more contemplative. I haven't changed a word. They convey my thoughts, feelings, and observations in the throes of my year-long trek along California's El Camino Real.

Enjoy!
Maggie

Tales from the Trail...

LEG ONE, DAY ONE

I began walking the El Camino Real mission trail today. The 800-mile historic road connects California's 21 Missions from San Diego to Sonoma, north of San Francisco. Hard-core hikers walk straight through, taking 55 days. I'm neither hard-core nor a true hiker, so I've divided the journey into twelve segments, walking one segment a month. I'm taking the opportunity to reconnect with family and friends during this expedition by having different people join me on each segment.

My buddy, Tracey, is walking with me on the first 75-mile leg over the next four days. The perfect way to start a trek of this magnitude is with a blessing from the priest at the Mission San Diego de Alcala.

Mission #1: San Diego de Alcalá

Tales from the Trail...

LEG ONE, DAY TWO

Our feet are feeling every step of the 45 miles we've covered so far. Motrin, Thermacare heat wraps, and Cliff bars kept us going. Blue skies and breezes off the Pacific Ocean propelled us north. Finished today's walk at the second Mission – beautiful San Luis Rey de Francia.

Mission #2: San Luis Rey de Francia

Tales from the Trail...

LEG ONE, DAY THREE

Our day started bright and early at the Oceanside Marina. Our 25-mile walk cut through Camp Pendleton military base. My friend, Captain Jim Reily, arranged clearance for us onto the huge 125,000-acre facility located between San Diego and Orange Counties. 37,000 troops live on the base. It's a self-contained city with housing developments, restaurants, schools, grocery stores, barbers, etc. A majority of the base is expansive, barren land. We ended today's hike at the San Clemente beach just in time for a gorgeous sunset.

Tales from the Trail...

LEG ONE, DAY FOUR

Our bodies were hurtin' this morning! Only ten miles remained for this segment of the El Camino Real hike. Fortified with moleskin, tape, and Bio Freeze, Tracey and I finished our four day, 80-mile walk at the Mission San Juan Capistrano. It's called the "Jewel of the Missions" because of its elaborate gardens,19th century bells, and many artifacts displayed throughout the grounds. Such a joy sharing this hiking experience with my good friend! We had lots of laughs along the way.

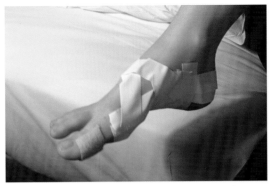

Mission #3: San Juan Capistrano

Tales from the Trail...

LEG TWO, DAY ONE – FOUR

Just returned from the second leg of my El Camino Real Mission walk. Hoofed the 68-mile trek solo from San Juan Capistrano to San Gabriel in LA.

Laguna Beach provided gorgeous Pacific Ocean views. During the four days, I passed through Anaheim, Newport Beach, Whittier, and more, with the scenery alternating from pretty to not pretty, pretty to not.

Lots of blisters on my feet. A pair of black suede, fleece-lined slippers from Walgreens eased the pain. I wore them for the last day of my walk – 17 miles. Surprised how well they held up! I should do a testimonial for the West Loop Bootie company!

This segment of the walk culminated at the San Gabriel Mission – one of the best preserved of all the missions. The alter was handcrafted in Mexico City in the 1790s and the baptismal font was a personal gift from King Carlos III of Spain. As with the four missions I've seen so far, it was gorgeous.

Mission #4: San Gabriel Arcángel

Tales from the Trail...

LEG THREE, DAY ONE

I've covered 164 of my 800-mile mission walk, so far. Feels like the tip of the iceberg :-). My good friend Cindy Freeman is joining me on this segment. A real trooper considering she's 62 with Parkinsons Disease. They shoot horses for less than that :-).

We started at the San Gabriel Mission, which led us onto Route 66. Loved the1950's signs and cultural landmarks. Culminated today's journey at our retro hotel, Safari Inn, an LA landmark where numerous movies and TV shows were filmed: Apollo 13, CSI, Desperate Housewives, The Closer, and Prison Break.

Ruminations from the Route...

LEG THREE, DAY TWO

Trekked through Northeast LA to San Fernando Rey de Espana Mission. Very ethnic area most of the 17-mile walk. Lots of yard sales and families selling homemade food.

The missions weren't constructed in sequential order from south to north. This is the 17th of the 21 Missions built. It's the 5th I've reached since leaving San Diego heading up the coast. The arches are its most prominent facade feature.

A wedding was taking place when Cindy and I arrived, so we had to wait to go inside. Bob and Dolores Hope are buried in the mission gardens.

A big plate of carbo-loaded Mexican food was the perfect dinner before we hit the hay.

Mission #5: San Fernando Rey de España

Ruminations from the Route...

LEG THREE, DAY THREE

Our feet are feeling the miles; covered 20 today. Glad I brought my slippers :-). Wearing them for tomorrow's walk. I added toe socks to my arsenal of pain management, as it does help with blisters.

Relieved to finally get out of LA and head into Ventura County. Horse ranches sit at the base of the mountains separating the two areas. Crossing over the two-lane Santa Susana Pass winding through the ridge was treacherous!! Cars flew by us as we traipsed through the brush on the side of the road. Nerve racking! As we reached the summit we took "selfies" and pics around the pass before starting the descent into Simi Valley.

Lots of John Wayne and Gene Autry western movies, as well as TV show's were filmed in the rocky hills: Fort Apache, Gunsmoke, Little House on the Prairie. Also, the Manson family lived there. Hanging in our hotel now watching our favorite show... Downton Abbey!

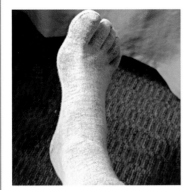

Santa Susana Pass

State Historic Park

CRAZY TRIGS RANCH
BOARDING · TRAINING · TLC

(818) 700-0039

Ruminations from the Route...

LEG THREE, DAY FOUR

Cindy did GREAT on this walk! Her goal was to prove to herself she can accomplish physical feats with Parkinsons. And that she did. The original plan was for her to walk two of the four days. She walked three: 55 miles!

I started the final day this morning after getting Cindy on the train to San Diego. The weather was perfect; sunny, in the 70's with a nice breeze. Simi Valley to Santa Rosa Valley and on into Camarillo was gorgeous! The 20-mile stretch passed exclusive developments with $2.6 million homes, agriculture fields sprouting celery and artichokes, and lemon groves that provide citrus to Sunkist. I understand why the entire area is called Pleasant Valley.

Before starting this year-long journey, my sister gave me an UP band to track my mileage and energy burned each day. The totals for this month's four day walk are: 167,093 steps, the equivalent of 75 miles, and 9,596 calories burned...probably the same amount I consumed, as well :-).

Getting my backpack lighter as the walk progresses helps when clocking this kind of mileage. I buy packages of cheap white tee shirts and undies from Costco and throw out the dirty ones each evening. Works great. I'm catching the Amtrak tomorrow morning. Ready to get home and see my hubby.

SANTA ROSA VALLEY
Children & Horses at Play
Drive Carefully

Sunkist
GROWER

Ruminations from the Route...

LEG FOUR, DAY ONE

My buddy Tami Dahl is joining me for this month's walk from Camarillo to Santa Barbara. We took Amtrak from San Diego last night. Gorgeous sunset as the silverbullet zoomed north along the coast. Arrived in Camarillo at 8:30 p.m. and walked to the nearby Bella Capri Inn. Cute hotel.

This morning's walk began where I left off last month – Pleasant Valley agriculture fields. Beautiful. Celery and strawberry plants reached to the horizon. Friendly migrant workers greeted us as we passed. Red berries were being boxed for Dole.

In the afternoon we veered west towards Oxnard Harbor. Views of ag fields were replaced by marinas and sailboats moored alongside waterfront homes.

Kurt and Rose Buckley, members of the California Mission Walkers' Facebook group, graciously invited Tami and I to stay at their house when they heard we were passing through their neck of the woods. Never met them, but we all became fast friends over stories of the trail. Rose had dinner ready for us when we arrived.

Kurt has walked the CA Mission trail in 53 days! No days off. He walked all day and camped at night – at the age of 72! He's walking with Tami and I tomorrow. He's training for an upcoming 250 mile "jaunt" on Spain's Camino de Santiago. I'll have to pick up the pace with Kurt along. Stay tuned...

Murmurs from the March...

LEG FOUR, DAY TWO

Day two began with Rose's delicious home–cooked breakfast. A real treat from the usual grab-and-go morning meals. Tami started the walk in Teva flip flops, trying to give her aching feet a break from the confines of her Reeboks. Kurt, the seasoned hiker, lead the way as we stormed Ventura's Harbor Boulevard fueled by copious cups of coffee. It was a welcome change to be following someone who knew the route vs. forging the path myself with Google maps and the hiker's guide. Within five miles Tami realized her rubber sandals wouldn't cut it on the El Camino Real. Luckily, she brought her sneaks. We reinforced her feet with moleskin and crammed her swollen feet into whatI'm sure felt like leather vises.

Ventura is flanked by two rivers – the Ventura and the Santa Clara – which mostly define its boundaries to the north and south. Where the latter river meets the Pacific Ocean sits a pretty estuary. A commune of pelicans, blue herons, and ducks leisurely glided around the open space.

Before long we entered Ventura Keys, an area of $1-2 million harborfront homes. We struck up a conversation with one of the residents whose wife runs the enclave's historical society. Fifty years ago the posh neighborhood was used as a waste dump alongside a small airport. Both were developed into the Keys, with home prices starting at $31,000. There was a line of people waiting to purchase the houses. And the rest, as they say, is history.

As we continued west towards the ocean to San Buenaventura State Park the marine layer began rolling in – a welcome reprieve from the sun. But, it did obstruct the full view of the Ventura Pier, which was constructed in 1872, making it one of California's oldest wooden piers.

From there, we turned directly east towards Main Street, home of the San Buenaventura Mission. Kurt has visited it numerous times, so he took a siesta on the park lawn across the street while Tami and I toured the historic landmark. As with all the churches, its buildings and gardens are beautiful. It is the ninth mission founded. A small thrift store named Two Women on a Mission sat by the entrance. Just as the name implied, there were a pair of sweet, elderly ladies running the shop. Both were knitting items to sell. Homemade breads, peanut brittle, resale clothing and jewelry were all for sale, with proceeds going to the mission. I couldn't resist a loaf of oatmeal soda bread. Never had it, but it sounded interesting. Going to have it for breakfast tomorrow.

The remaining five miles of the day took us along the ocean. We hopped a set of railroad tracks to get closer to the water. As if on cue, the sun began setting, casting a gorgeous sheen on the Pacific. Rose picked us up at Solimar Beach – a surfers hangout. Dinner was at a nearby Japanese restaurant. Tempura hit the spot after a 14–mile walk. We bid our fabulous hosts Kurt and Rose adieu tomorrow and meet up with another California Mission Walker who just happens to be named Curt, as well. He's accompanying Tami and I to Carpinteria. Let me tell ya, a girl could get used to these personal guides :-).

Mission #6: San Buenaventura

Murmurs from the March...

LEG FOUR, DAY THREE

After our goodbyes to Kurt and Rose, Tami and I met up with another CA Mission Walker – Curt Cragg. He's an avid mountain hiker who decided to tackle the El Camino Real to test his distance endurance with the high milage days required on the mission walk. In the 1980s as a young guy in his 20s, Curt had mapped out a bicycling trip of the ECR, but his tour never came to fruition. Fast forward 30 years and he's fulfilling his original goal, only now on foot.

Most of the day we walked on the hard packed beach sand. Wonderful! The ocean breezes kept us cool. A few spots were overtaken with basketball sized rocks we scrambled across. A local man said two weeks ago the rocks were not there. The tide had washed them in! We detoured to the 101 bypass a few times to avoid these areas. Cement barriers had recently been installed on the busy road, providing protection from oncoming traffic. Hallelujah!

The straight shot up the coast didn't require much navigation so our attention was directed on spotting unique seashells and other treasures. Quite a few oil platforms sit on the horizon of the Pacific Ocean. Curt said they are mostly between Ventura County and Santa Barbara.

About 2:30 p.m. we turned onto the main drag of Carpinteria, our stop for today's walk. Before Curt continued on to his home in Santa Ynez Valley, we thanked him for putting up with two, slow-movin' girls. As a wilderness guide for REI, he assured us he's accustomed to tapering his pace. Tami and I hoofed the few remaining blocks to our hotel, taking in the sights, signs, and sounds of the small community.

Pondering from the Path...

LEG FOUR, DAY FOUR

Yesterday was the final day for this leg of the walk. It began with Tami and I on a dirt walkway skirting the railroad tracks precariously close, hobo-style, for half a mile. It spilled onto Santa Claus Lane, a street lined with boutique shops. After a few purchases we continued on toward Santa Barbara. In no time we were among multi- million dollar compounds on a beautiful tree-lined road. Kevin Costner is said to live in one of them. Perhaps the one we saw with the seashell-covered mailbox.

Before our route turned onto the beach, Tami exchanged her sneakers for slippers. At this point she was questioning her sanity. Before long, we ascended to Lookout Park on the bluffs overlooking the Pacific Ocean. While relaxing there we met a family of six – four kids under the age of five, including a set of ten month old twin girls – who were driving from Alaska to Cabo, Mexico! And I thought I was crazy!! Not far from here, in Summerland, Tami cried uncle and said she was DONE. She called a cab, which drove her eight miles to the mission.

Needless to say, the remaining portion of the walk wasn't as fun without Tami. I put my nose to the grindstone and continued on to Montecito – home to Oprah and the Four Seasons Biltmore Hotel, owned by Ty Warner, founder of Beanie Babies. Here's where I met the final section of beach, which escorted me to Santa Barbara. Numerous people were sifting sand looking for beach glass to make jewelry. Dogs played fetch, pelicans preened at the waters edge, and hang-gliders soared overhead.

As I approached Santa Barbara city center there was a large sculpture installed as an homage to their LGBT community. Stearns Wharf was bustling with tourists. From here I had a two-mile uphill climb to the mission. When I arrived, Tami was sitting on a bench reading People magazine. We toured the Santa Barbara Mission, nicknamed Queen of the Missions. Chumash Indians built it in the 1790's. Museum artifacts displayed the native's currency and decorations.

Lodging last night was at Auto Camp, a village of vintage Airstream trailers exquisitely restored as "hotel rooms." Very cool! (www.SBAutoCamp.com). We're on Amtrak now heading back to San Diego. Tune in next month for the continuation of my El Camino Real mission walk.

Chumash Money. Made from olivella shells by Chumash on Santa Cruz Island. Donated by Karl Oscar Borg in 1921. Likely prior to 1800.

Mission #7: Santa Barbara

Visions from the Venture...

LEG FIVE, DAY ONE

My posse is growing! Roxanna, a Delta flight attendant friend of mine; Dorinda, one of her co-workers; Louie, my brother-in-law; and Jim, a member of the California Mission Walkers, all signed up for the Santa Barbara to Orcutt leg. Jim, who none of us had met before, lives in nearby Buellton. He and his wife Sharon graciously opened their home to us for this segment of the trip. The camaraderie among mission hikers is heartwarming and amazing.

The mission where I finished last month was our starting point. As always, we began the day with pep in our step and enthusiasm to take on the El Camino Real. It wasn't long before we were on the beach. We threw our arms wide open and said "this is fabulous!" Within a mile the hard packed sand turned into rocks, and our leisurely stroll became work. The tide was coming in, eating at our dry land. Soon our only option was to let the waves hit us as we climbed over huge boulders covered in tar. Apparently, in this area, the black goo seeps up from the earth depositing huge formations and covering boulders.

Maneuvering the obstacles was tiring! These rocky conditions continued for most of our 17-mile hike. The only break came when we scaled a set of rickety stairs and cut through the UCSB campus on the cliffs above...which, by the way, is a college student's dream location!

We skirted the bluffs on a dirt path, making our way back down to the beach where the campus fed into a highway. We eventually got to a point where the tides and rocks made the area impassable. We ascended the bluffs again to a small pocket park overlooking the Pacific. Because the freeway was to the east and the ocean overtook the beach walk to the west, we had no option but to finish for the day. To be honest, no one was disappointed. Sharon came to our rescue and we arrived at the house wet, sandy, and hungry. After dinner at a nearby restaurant, we fell into bed and slept like rocks.

Fodder from the Footpath...

LEG FIVE, DAY TWO

Day two tested our stamina to the nth degree! Leaving El Capitan State Beach, we veered east and headed into the Los Padres National Forest via Refugio Pass that gained 2,600 feet in elevation. Doesn't sound too bad until you add sun, 85 degrees, and lots of switch-backs! The payoff was spectacular views of the Channel Islands clustered miles out in the Pacific Ocean. Refugio Pass is home to Ronald Reagan's Western White House. Nancy donated the ranch to the Young Republicans, who now use it as a retreat.

We descended into the Santa Ynez Valley, passing horse farms and vineyards. One corral had a zebra grazing alongside a donkey. Jim said it may be an adopted pet from nearby "Neverland," Michael Jackson's past home.

After a pit stop at El Rancho Market for ice cold water, we powered to the Santa Inez Mission as the sun set. We cut through a field to our final destination and came upon a beautifully lit mission with its doors open, greeting parishioners for 7 p.m. mass. Sweaty, smelly, and beat, we fell into the pews, fixated on the gorgeous alter before us, and gave thanks for the safe 24-mile journey we'd just completed.

Mission #8: Santa Inés

Gabbing from the Ground...

LEG FIVE, DAY THREE

This month's walk has such diverse topography. The first day was on the beach. Second day was over a mountain. Third day we marched for 19 miles along the monotonous, straight route 246 from Santa Inez Mission to La Parisima Mission in Lompoc. Jim stayed home nursing a nasty blister. He lives in the area, so he'd already walked this section of the El Camino Real.

Rox, Dorinda, Louie, and I toured the Santa Inez Mission before heading out about 9:45 a.m. Along the way we took in the Santa Ynez and Buellton roadside attractions. We hadn't been walking long when we came upon an ostrich and emu farm! Rox and I couldn't resist a quick visit with our feisty feathered friends. The $4 admission fee was money well spent, as was $16 for a bottle of emu oil.

Next break was a few miles down the road at a lavender farm. Among fields of purple blooms sat a small shed where a grandpa and his grandson were selling lavender creams, soaps, oils, etc. Rox purchased enough goodies to warrant shipping to her home in Seattle, WA. The 90- year old man and his 40-something scion were a hoot! Grandpa couldn't believe we were walking 19 miles in one day, let alone 800 over the course of a year.

Soon the shops waned and Santa Rita Hills appellation with its bucolic vineyards flanked the road. The movie "Sideways" was filmed at this popular wine destination. Seemed like a good place to rest on the grass and eat the picnic we'd been carrying. Plus, the sole of Louie's hiking boot fell off, so the stop was two-fold. Good thing Dorinda had her size 11 Tevas along, which could be adjusted to fit Louie's feet. He muddled through the remaining miles in women's sandals.

We arrived at La Purisima Concepcion Mission as the sun was setting over nearby spinach fields. Beautiful! Jim was so sweet to be waiting at the entrance to shuttle us to his house for a hot shower, followed by dinner with he and Sharon at Firestone Taproom. Delicious way to end the day.

Gabbing from the Ground...

LEG FIVE, DAY FOUR

By the 4th day of this month's walk my amigos were dropping like flies. Jim, Louie, and Dorinda opted out of the final 15 miles, leaving Rox and I to forge ahead. We left La Purisima Concepcion via a dirt path, and within minutes we were lost :-). The trail had numerous arteries leading in different directions. After walking in circles for awhile we saw a cowgirl and her horse ride up over the ridge. She pointed us in the right direction and we were on our way. Signs for mountain lions and rattle snakes encouraged vigilance as we picked up the pace :-).

Another mountain pass waited up ahead, although this time not nearly as steep or long. It transported us from Lompoc into the Santa Maria Valley. We then arrived at the crossroads of route 135 & Harris Grade Road. Nothing but farmland. The original plan of taking a cab to our hotel was not an option because there was no address to give the taxi company. So, we reverted to plan B... hitchhiking :-).

As we stood among the freshly tilled soil, a farm manager and a migrant worker pulled up to survey the acres' planting conditions. We asked for a ride to the nearest restaurant so we could call a cab. Roberto, the manager, was so nice and offered to take us directly to our hotel nine miles away. But, just in case, I got out my pepper spray and concealed it in my hand. We learned Roberto has worked on the farm for 20 years. He worked his way up to manager. His wife and three kids live in Morelia, MX, where he sends money to support them. Once a year he heads south and visits his family.

We arrive in downtown Santa Maria, small town USA. Flyers hung on electrical polls advertising city events including a pickle ball tournament – a combo of tennis, badminton, and ping pong. Our hotel was cool! Built in 1817, it hosted numerous stars through the years: Bob Hope, Jack Lemon, presidents, etc. Rox and I stayed in a room once occupied by Mickey Rooney. We had a delicious dinner by the fireplace in the hotel restaurant. Then off to bed early. I've now completed the 5th leg of my mission walk. Seven segments to go. Ugh...

Mission #9: La Purisima Concepción

Agony from the Acres...

LEG SIX, DAY ONE

It's with a heavy heart I start this months mission walk. My Dad passed away in March. He was 83. A stroke took him after years of battling Parkinsons Disease. I used to telephone Dad on my walks telling him what scenery I was passing at the time. I miss him.

I didn't walk in April, so this month I'm covering twice the mileage. Ugh. I started today in Guadalupe where I left off in March. It's just me and my shadow for the first two days until I meet up with my friend Jim.

Within the first quarter mile of today's walk I passed a cemetery. With a lump in my throat, I continued on towards the Rancho Guadalupe Dunes Preserve, 592 acres of pristine sand, crashing waves, and blue sky – the trifecta of beauty. More than 115 rare plant and animal species inhabit the refuge. Except for the few fishermen casting for surfperch, the beach was deserted. Surprising, given the 97-degree heat!

I hit a snag at Oso Flaco. The stretch in front of Santa Maria Refinery was closed to the public. A detour inland and then back to the beach in Oceano a few miles north was the only route for walkers.

Smooth sailing from Oceano to Pismo Beach. The area was open to autos, bicycles, dogs, even horses, as was evident with the horse hoof imprints near the waters edge. Sand dollars littered the beach and kids played in the surf.

The Pismo Beach Pier was hopping. A farmers market sat at the entrance to the pier. I never tasted such good watermelon juice! Cottage Inn by the Sea is home for the night. Views of the Pacific from my guest room are breathtaking!

Agony from the Acres...

LEG SIX, DAY TWO

One word describes today's walk - HOT! 102 degrees hot! But, I digress. The day started wonderfully. From my hotel room patio I watched two gray whales breach in the crystal blue ocean as they migrated north for the summer. A dolphin was leading the way, surfacing with the whales every so often. Truly spectacular!

My hotel was buzzing with participants of the Amgen bicycle race. Pismo Beach Pier was the starting line for the 5th leg of the competition. The hotel parking lot was swarming with buff men and women in spandex and their support vehicles from all over the world.

I wrapped my toes with moleskin, put on my compression socks, and headed north around 8 a.m. Shell Beach was 10 minutes up the road. It's a speck of a town along side the 101. The motels' old neon signs were reminiscent of the 1950s. Small ma and pa cafés lined the streets.

About two miles outside of the quintessential beach town I headed east towards the Mission San Luis Obispo de Tolosa. In no time the temps began to climb. My iPhone read 100 degrees and it felt like it. I poured water over my head to keep cool. Within minutes it was evaporated. I stopped in the shade numerous times as 100 degrees turned to 102. It was stifling! Slowly but surely I reached the mission having covered only about 10 miles today.

San Luis Obispo – or SLO as the locals call it – is halfway between Los Angeles and San Francisco. It was recently featured as the Happiest Town in America in the National Geographic book "Thrive". I happen to be here on the biggest night of the week – Farmers Market night. Three blocks of Higuera St. becomes pedestrian only and vendors line both sides. A bike valet will "park" your bike for free as you indulge in a triple chocolate dipped Twinkie; or break open your own geode; or have your dreams interpreted. I think I know why it's the happiest town...these people are stoned!!!! :-).

A few blocks from the market is gum alley. The long narrow passage is covered in chewed gum! Tourists flock here to get photos of themselves sticking chewed gum among the thousands of other pieces of chewed gum... gross!!

I headed back to the Granada Hotel early. It's a cool, 1922 property that used to be a brothel. An investment group named The Lunacy Club renovated the building, modernizing the look and updating all plumbing and electric, but kept the integrity of brick walls and old guest room door keys. Ironically, the keys are made by Baldwin in Reading, PA, located about 35 miles from my hometown, Lancaster, PA. Small world.

I'm hitting the hay soon. Meeting my friend, Jim, at the SLO Mission at 6:30 a.m. We're starting our walk early to try and beat the heat. We have an 18-mile day tomorrow. Yikes!

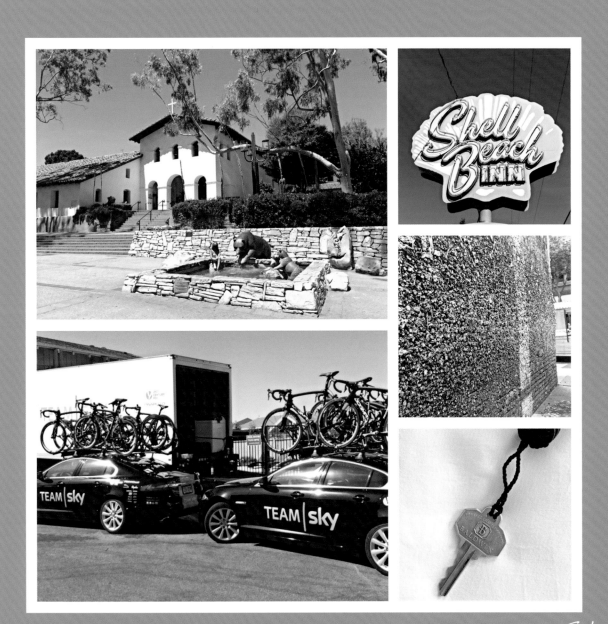

Mission #10: San Luis Obispo de Tolosa

Rustlings from the Road...

LEG SIX, DAY THREE

My buddy, Jim, met me at the SLO mission. I arrived early to get photos of the circa 1772 structure in the morning light. One of the 550 El Camino Real bells sits at the entrance. It was dedicated to the city on November 25, 1909.

The heat subsided considerably today. Ocean breezes coaxed us west to Morro Bay for our 18-mile hike. After weaving through numerous SLO neighborhoods, we were on a main artery heading out of the city. Cars whizzed by us as we hugged the shoulder. While focusing on the oncoming traffic, I failed to see a big snake camouflaged in the roadside brush. Luckily I didn't step on him, but it did elicit a scream from me :-). I snapped a quick photo and took off running!

Before long we turned onto a quiet two lane road void of traffic. We strolled past fields of wheat, fava beans, and sugar peas before merging onto dirt paths winding through tall evergreens and Spring wildflowers. We reached Morro Bay by 2 p.m. and it was breezy enough to wear a jacket. Hard to believe 24 hours prior it was over 100 degrees.

Dinner was on the bay at The Great American Fish Company overlooking Morro Rock – for which the city is named. The volcanic mass was formed 23 million years ago and is 576 feet tall. It's often called the Gibraltar of the Pacific. Morro means "crown shape hill." The rock became a state landmark in 1968 and is designated as a bird sanctuary for the Peregrine Falcon and other species.

Tomorrow takes us 23 miles east to Paso Robles. Another early start will be necessary. We're thinking it will be a 9-1/2 hour trek. Stay tuned...

Howls from the Hoof...

LEG SIX, DAY FOUR

As Jim and I left this morning, a marine layer shrouded Morro Rock in the distance. Egrets splashed among seaweed-covered beach rocks as we traipsed the sand heading to Paso Robles. The weather was cool. All was good. Then we headed east over Old Creek Road, a 10-mile, two-lane, windy mountain pass with NO SHOULDER! It's here we both concluded I'm a scaredy-cat :-). Jim wasn't conerned about the walking conditions. I, on the other hand, was convinced we were going to be run over. At this point I questioned whether the mission walk was adventurous or foolish.

I placated myself by saying if it gets too treacherous we can hitchhike to our destination. Some passerby would surely take pity on us and stop. Onward and upward we trekked. It's amazing how quickly adrenaline propels one forward. My eyes were glued to the road. Whenever I heard the roar of an engine I'd yell "car" to Jim who was walking ahead of me single file. He didn't flinch as it zoomed passed. I'd throw myself into the hillside, emerging covered in foxtails and weeds. Water consumption had to be monitored. There was no place to fill our jugs while on this stretch.

The few times I allowed myself to take in the scenery Mother Nature's beauty surrounded us. Towering trees, wild turkeys foraging among poppy flowers, and fields of yellow mustard plants. Folklore claims centuries ago Padres marked the El Camino Real by spreading mustard seed along the road as they built the mission chain. Because field mustard grows all over California it's unlikely true, but it's a fun story.

We arrived in Paso tired, hot, hungry, thirsty, and stressed (at least I was). Hallelujah, we'd made it! Rocky Creek Cellars was the first sign of civilization. Paso's known for it's vineyards, with 270 wineries lining the long main drag. BBQ was cooking and music was playing. We limped up the driveway, bought 2 big bottles of ice cold water and plopped down on the patio chairs. Another 17 miles completed.

I'm finding Central California's hiking infrastructure to be more challenging. Pedestrian dirt trails and sidewalks are limited, requiring mission walkers to traverse less than optimal roads. Until I reach the developed areas of Monterey, Carmel, and north, isolated and hazardous sections will be more frequent.

Tomorrow is day 5 of this months walk. It's 11 miles to the San Miguel Mission. I'm a bit trepidatious after today....

Musings from My Meandering...

LEG SIX, DAY FIVE

Surprisingly, my old bod feels fairly good for starting the fifth consecutive day of walking. Motrin is my friend. Only one small blister. A double layer of moleskin remedied the problem.

The 11 miles to Mission San Miguel Arcangel were beautiful. Jim and I met at Starbucks in the morning. We stayed at different hotels last night. He opted for Budget Inn. I needed a little pampering. La Bellasera Hotel & Suites fit the bill. Puffy duvets and room service.

My 7:45 a.m. cab request was a no show. Paso's taxis don't start running till 11 a.m. They cater to the late night wine drinking crowd instead. But, small town hospitality prevailed when the hotel's college age bellboy offered to drive me to Starbucks in his truck.

The day's path took Jim and I passed vineyards, a bamboo farm, freshly-plowed grain fields, and horses. Jim's savant knowledge of botany kept me entertained as he recited local flora genus facts. Who knew wild tobacco was so pretty with its large white blooms! Jim surmised it was used in Native American peace pipes, but suggested I fact check his statement.

We arrived at the mission as mass was ending. The historic structure resides in a rural, one-horse town. No stop lights. No grocery store. Just a small market. The preservation of the mission is remarkable. An earthquake in 2003 nearly demolished it, forcing parishioners to worship outside for five years while the sanctuary was painstakingly restored. Today, wall cracks are the only vestiges of the seismic occurrence. We got a true sense of what the mission looked like when first built in 1797. The tower's 2000-pound bell still rings daily.

After a pizza lunch we caught the only bus going through town. Line 9 took me to Paso and Jim to SLO where he left his car on Friday. He and our friend, Curt, who Tami and I walked with in Ventura, are meeting me on Thursday for another five-day hike. It's too far for me to return home and come north again in 3 days. I'm hanging out in Central California taking a breather before the next march. Hopefully I can find a good masseuse :-).

Mission #11: San Miguel Arcángel

On the Road Again...

LEG SEVEN, DAY ONE

Started the seventh leg of my mission walk today after a much needed three-day break in San Luis Obispo. I hung out in the hotel room, read, ate, and watched QVC home shopping network.

Today's 6-1/2 mile walk was perfect to ease me back onto the road. I'm trekking 10 days this month, so a short day is appreciated. I'm joined by my friends Jim and Curt.

We reached the Mission San Antonio this afternoon. Number 12 for me of the 21 total Missions. Interestingly, it's located on Fort Hunter Liggett military base in South Monterey County. Of the 162,000 acres owned by the government, the mission sits on 86 acres of private land. This came to be years ago when William Randolph Hearst owned all the land, including the mission. He sold the entire kit--and- kaboodle to the government, at which time the mission became privately owned. Its Parrish is tiny, consisting of only 33 families. Two full-time employees and a sweet, black cat run the place.

The mission grounds have 29 guest rooms where the public can stay. Reservations must be made well in advance, so we're staying at the Hacienda on the base. It's a cool 1929 abode built by Hearst to house 30 ranch employees. It was designed by architect Julia Morgan, the same woman who designed Hearst Castle in San Simeon.

Guests retrieve their room key from a lock box using a code. Barebones customer service. Curt is staying in one of the Cowboy rooms where guests must share a bathroom at the end of a long outdoor corridor. Not me! I booked a Tower room with private bath. Jim did too. Well worth the extra $35! Food options are pizza at the base bowling alley, or bring your own – which we did. A relaxing cookout on Curt's portable grill was the perfect end to the day.

ON MARCH 6, 1776 LT. COL. JUAN
BAUTISTA DE ANZA ARRIVED AT THIS
MISSION ON HIS FAMOUS OVERLAND
EXPEDITION FROM SONORA, MEXICO,
TO MONTEREY AND SAN FRANCISCO.
HE WAS ACCOMPANIED BY 240 COLON-
ISTS & THE DIARIST, PADRE PEDRO
FONT, WHO WROTE THE INDIANS OF
THIS MISSION ARE TOTALLY DISTINCT
FROM THOSE I HAVE HITHERTO SEEN.
HE RECORDED THE PLACE AS MISSION
SAN ANTONIO IN THE VALLEY OF
THE OAKS.

6 ESPACIO D'EL Peregrino

Mission #12: San Antonio de Padua

Insights from the Insanity...

LEG SEVEN, DAY TWO

An early start was imperative today with temps expected to reach the mid-90s. A whole lot of nothing stretched along our two-lane road from Lake San Antonio to Fort Hunter Liggett. For those who worry about California's overdevelopment, they need only visit the central coast's inland communities. Acres and acres of open land flank country roads with only the occasional farm. Birds sing. Squirrels frolic. Except for the cars zipping by, it's a bucolic setting.

Curt's pace was head and shoulders faster than Jim and I. Within minutes he was a dot on the horizon way ahead of us. To pass the time we identified local birds...western blue jays, red wing blackbirds...and...turkey vultures!! They circled above us as we sidestepped carcasses picked clean along the roadside.

We walked 13 miles till reaching the Lockwood Store to replenish our water supply. It's the only game in town, so people were coming and going. Curt arrived 30 minutes before us, so he was ready to leave and knock out the remaining 6 miles for the day. Jim and I bid him adieu and sat down for lunch. The diner was decorated in nostalgic tin signs. One of them depicting a bygone soda, Mission Orange Beverage.

By 3:30 p.m. we caught up with Curt at our destination. Nineteen miles in 95-degree heat and hot winds had whooped me. Thank God we're staying at the Hacienda again tonight! My boxed breakfast they supply in the guest room fridge awaits me for the start of tomorrow's journey.

Insights from the Insanity...

LEG SEVEN, DAY THREE

At 4:30 a.m. the alarm pulled me out of bed to start the 8th day of my May mission walk. Having covered 115 miles since I arrived in Central California last week, it's getting harder to coax myself from the warm pillowy down. My left foot has more blisters than not. One on the heel. One on the ball. One between the toes. The list goes on.

It was a gorgeous morning! Sun shining and a cool breeze. Within the first mile we came upon the dilapidated historic Dutton Hotel. It was built by Antonio Ramirez in 1849 along El Camino Real between Mission San Antonio and Mission Soledad. George Dutton became owner in 1878. He added a store and saloon. The thoroughfare where the hotel sits was a major artery to the gold fields of California. But, by 1886 the railroad bypassed the area and the original El Camino Real fell into disrepair. The hotel was added to the National Register of Historic Places in the 1970s.

Natural beauty accompanied us most the way today. Spanish moss dripped from enormous oak trees. Deer hopped across grassy meadows. An early morning start allows us to see more wildlife.

By mile 10 my left foot was in pain and I was holding Jim back. I told him to go ahead, but he's too much of a gentleman to leave me behind. I decided to catch a ride to our King City hotel. As luck would have it, two women we met at the Hacienda last night told us they were driving to King City the next day for gasoline, taking the same road we were walking. So, when they passed us, I hitched a ride :-).

Not long after I arrived at Motel 6 — one of only two hotels in town — Curt completed the day's walk. His pace is amazing. Jim wasn't far behind. I am so out of my league hiking with both these guys.

An early dinner at Wildhorse Cafe hit the spot. It's amazing how good food tastes after walking miles. A trip to Rite Aid was necessary to reassess my blister care. My current remedy has been rendered useless after covering this much pavement. Hopefully the addition of micropour tape and hydrocolloid adhesive will do the trick. Plus...my slippers! Yup, it's time to pull out the fleece .

Nonsense from My Noodle...

LEG SEVEN, DAY FOUR

I fortified my foot with hikers armor and took off at 7 a.m. Jim, Curt, and I traveled through Central Valley's salad bowl today. Stop and go, stop and go was our MO as we weaved among veggie fields taking photos. Cauliflower, carrots, Spring Mix lettuce, and onion fields laid at the base of distant golden hills. I loved meandering through the cropland.

The 16-mile day was slow and steady. El Camino Real's ubiquitous mustard flower lead the way over Metz Road pass to our Greenfield destination. So peaceful.

When descending into the field workers' community we came upon Espinosa Road. Had to stop for a photo op. Budget Inn is home for the evening. It's a flea bag, but there's no other option. We leave tomorrow morning at 6 a.m. for Soledad Mission; the final day of my May mission walk! Yahoo!!

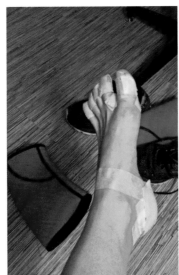

Tales from My Toes...

LEG SEVEN, DAY FIVE

The May segment of my California mission walk is complete. Elation surged through my body as we reached Mission Nuestra Señora de la Soledad. Two sweet elderly women running the gift shop greeted us with big smiles.

The last day's walk was one of the most gorgeous since starting in Guadalupe 145 miles ago. Monterey Wine Country was our backdrop for the five-hour jaunt to the mission. J. Lohr vineyard's sprawling 1,100 acres went on for miles. Syrah and Chardonnay grapes seemed the most prolific. Zabala and Ventana vineyards were keeping up with the big guy. The sun's rays cast off the verdant leaves; a photographers dream. No way our smart phones could capture the beauty.

We polished off the last of our many Kind energy bars. After consuming cases over the 10 day walk I've dubbed them Unkind bars! I feel the same about Gatorade, too. Sustenance on the road gets mundane.

While walking the dirt paths I found a little wooden heart on the ground. My father passed away 10 weeks ago. I thought about him often on this month's journey. Ironically, he was a cardiologist and it was a heart I found. Perhaps a little gift from him.

May's walk was by far the most challenging, as of yet. My Dad's death, the heat, the mileage, the number of days, and the painful feet all played a part. My physical and mental fortitude were tested. There were times I wanted to cry. Or wanted to scream. Or both. I am so grateful for my fellow peregrinos, Jim and Curt. Their companionship, good humor, and route directions were priceless. We consumed Central California's spectacular scenery and met wonderful people along our trail. I'm on Amtrak now heading home. Can't wait to see my husband and my dog.

Mission #13: Nuestra Señora de la Soledad

Mutterings from Monterey...

LEG EIGHT, DAY ONE

As my sister said when I told her I was off on the 8th leg of my mission walk..."already???" Yes, I've hit the road once again. This months victims, er, co-walkers :-) are three women I've never met. They contacted me via the California Mission Walkers' Facebook page expressing interest in joining me on the El Camino Real. Sitting left to right in the accompanying photo are Genette from Pasadena, Sheryl from San Luis Obispo, me, and Peggy from San Diego.

Six o'clock yesterday morning Peggy and I caught Amtrak for a 12-hour trip north to Soledad where I ended last month's walk. Genette got on board in LA. With no photo to identify her, we watched for a backpack laden woman roaming the aisle of the Coast Starlight train.

The remainder of the ride we all swapped life stories and hiking adventures while watching the scenery whiz by from the glass ceiling viewing car.

Because of Sheryl's close proximity to Salinas she drove and met us at the station. Her Facebook photo helped me recognize her among the throngs of people on the platform.

None of the women have walked the California mission trail. But, both Sheryl and Genette have tackled Europe's Camino de Santiago – a pilgrimage route to the shrine of the apostle St. James the Great. Approximately 200,000 people attempt the 500-mile journey annually starting at the French border, going over the Pyrenees Mountains and into Spain. It takes an average of 33 days, walking 15 miles a day. I told my husband if I EVER express interest in attempting Santiago please say no and tie me to a chair :-).

Our day's walk from Soledad to Chualar (pronounced chew-lar) passed through Gonzales, where we stopped for lunch. With only 16 miles to cover we could take our time.

Since starting my walk in San Diego I've carried a Pilgrims Credential booklet, which I get stamped when entering each mission, as well as collect fun stickers and business cards from places I visit. As of today, I've filled the booklet. I'll start a second "passport," which it's sometimes called, tomorrow.

Next up, Chualar to Salinas. Then west to Carmel — with Sheryl Collmer and Margaret Johnston.

Tidbits from My Travels...

LEG EIGHT, DAY TWO

The four amigas are dwindling. Genette's battling a cold and decided she's better off home in bed than on the trail. The 8:45 a.m. Amtrak shuttled her back to Pasadena.

Sheryl is nursing a painful post surgery ankle, so she decided to sit today out. That left Peggy and I to continue on to Salinas – John Steinbeck country.

The Grapes of Wrath came to life as we walked passed farm workers harvesting romain lettuce. They, like the books protagonist Tom Joad, have come to California seeking a better life.

Women were washing crops seconds after being pulled from the soil. The immigrants cover themselves head to toe for protection from the elements...both natural and man made. Peggy and I were taken aback when we came upon many planted fields displaying signs with a skull and crossbones reading "DANGER: Pesticide. Do Not Enter." Hummm, may be a good reason to buy organic.

After 10 miles we joined Sheryl for lunch at Dubber's Sport Bar to refuel with veggie burgers and iced tea while watching TV cheering on Germany and Ghana in the World Cup.

Afterwards, we fit in a quick tour of the John Steinbeck Center/Museum before resuming our walk. It won't come as a surprise that Travels With Charley is one of my favorite novels of the Nobel Prize writer. It's a travelogue depicting Steinbeck's road trip around the United States in a camper with his standard poodle, Charley. Perhaps my bichon frise and I need to write a sequel... Travels With Marcel :-).

Treasures from My Trek...

LEG EIGHT, DAY THREE

Today's walk was beu-tee-full !!! Our sinuous trail wound through Fort Ord National Monument. The former United States Army post closed in 1994 after 77 years of functioning as a maneuver area and field artillery target range.

It later reopened as part of the National Landscape Conservation System. Two years ago President Obama designated the 14,651 acre parcel to its current status. The endangered Smith's blue butterfly, Contra Costa goldfields wildflower, and California Tiger Salamander ensure Ord's nature reserve status for many years to come.

A labyrinth of paths escort hikers and mountain bikers throughout the public park. Blue skies and golden hills accompanied Sheryl, Peggy, and I; postcard perfect vistas around every corner.

Our planned route had us skirt the park's southern portion, but a closer look at the map revealed a more scenic walk diagonally across the grounds towards Monterey Peninsula. A few hours into the hike our deviation hit a snag. By this I mean locked gates. Turning back wasn't an option – too far. So we hopped the fences and squeezed through when possible :-). It's going to take more of a roadblock to hold us back. Like a trip to jail for hiking off the designated trails :-).

By 4 p.m. we reached our destination – the small town of Del Rey Oaks. Once again, a California Mission Walker member has offered to host me and my hiking partners while in Monterey/Carmel county. Bob Brunson and his family opened their guest casita to us for two nights. The generosity I've experienced from complete strangers since I started my hike 550 miles ago has been so heartwarming! Dinner with the Brunson's at a nearby restaurant was a treat. Wonderful people.

Tomorrow is a short, eight-mile walk to Mission Carmel, so the girls and I are going to sleep in. Yay!!

Babble from the Broad...

LEG EIGHT, DAY FOUR

GORGEOUS is the only way to describe the final day of this month's walk! Bob's wife, Teresa, took the navigation reins and lead Sheryl, Peggy, and I on the eight mile walk to Mission San Carlos Borrome de Carmelo. We were off by the crack of 9:45 a.m. :-). So nice to sleep in and not hit the road early.

We caught the east side of the 17-Mile Drive, a scenic road through Pebble Beach and Pacific Grove on the Monterey Peninsula. Within minutes towering coastal oaks and pines surrounded us. Tree trunks shot to the sky, their enormity humbling.

Our path spilled onto Carmel's pristine, white sand shore. This pocket beach has no sediment from creeks, creating this jewel. The craggy coast went on for miles. Monterey Cypress dotted the cliffs. Click, click, click went our cameras. Wow, was this head-and-shoulders easier than jumping fences in Fort Ord around the Laguna Seca Raceway :-).

By 1 p.m. we arrived at the mission. Junipero Serra, the Spanish Franciscan friar who founded the first nine of California's missions, is buried at Carmel. His remains are under the altar, but a sepulcher venerating him fills a room in the mission museum.

We attended mass, all the while mesmerized by the religious iconography around us. Afterwards, we approached the priest asking if he had a blessing for sore feet :-). He had a great sense of humor, laughing as we discussed the miracles of Epson Salt :-). Placing his hands on my shoulders he prayed for the safe continuation of my journey.

Sheryl drove back to San Luis Obispo. Peggy and I stayed at the Cypress Inn, Doris Day's historic hotel in downtown Carmel. Interior walls are covered with her movie posters, and her old films played on TVs. It's pet-friendly. Dogs of all sizes, from huge great danes to little chihuahuas, roamed the hallways. Doris just celebrated her 90th birthday. She lives close by in the valley.

After a good night sleep my co-walker and I boarded the silver bullet south this morning to San Diego.

Mission #14: San Carlos Borroméo del Carmelo

Regales from the Trails...

LEG NINE, DAY ONE

Started the ninth leg of my Mission walk today in Monterey. My darling nephews are joining me from different ends of the USA: 11-year old Gabe from Seattle, and 28-year old Pete from Philadelphia. Add my good friend Jim and we have a hiking quartet pounding the path this month.

Today's nine-miler to Marina was the perfect distance. Wish the entire El Camino could be tackled in such small bites, but it would take too long to complete. Pete had a morning meeting in Philly, so he couldn't join us till tonight. Gabe, Jim, and I warmed up the trail for him. We spent 3-1/2 hours strolling along the Monterey Bay Sanctuary Scenic Trail at Fort Ord Dunes. This is the western edge of the Fort Ord monument Peggy, Sheryl, and I hiked thru last month.

Once a United States Army installation during WW II and the Vietnam War, the trail opened in 2009 and still has remnants of its past life. One of the original 15 firing stations still stands, as well as storage bunkers dug into the dunes where ammunition was once kept. Graffiti covers the facades.

We finished our walk early, giving Gabe and I time to visit the Monterey Bay Aquarium. Jim's been there so many times with his wife and two daughters he opted to pass. Over 35,000 creatures fill the aquarium's 34 galleries. Construction cost $55 million. There are over 200 exhibits offering a glimpse into the underwater world. Gabe and I could have spent days staring at the beautiful sea life. The staff had to kick us out at the 6 p.m. closing time.

Back we went to the home of our dear friends Bob and Teresa who graciously opened their spare guest flat to my co-walkers and I again. The girls and I stayed here a couple days last month. Now I'm back for two nights with a new group of hikers. I'm getting to be a regular :-). Plus, the Brunson's lent me their car to pick up Pete at the airport. You'll be hard-pressed to meet a nicer family.

Regales from the Trails...

LEG NINE, DAY TWO

The boys and I bid adios to Salinas and headed to the next town, San Juan Bautista. Nice having my other nephew Pete folded into the group for today's 18-mile walk.

The central valleys ubiquitous veggie fields waned as we traversed Old Stage Road. The dirt path once serviced Wells Fargo coaches. Rows of lettuce and strawberries segued into oak-lined foothills of the De Anza Trail; lush, green, and gorgeous!

Our seven hour hike was peppered with fun hypothetical questions..."if you had a time machine would you rather go back or forward 200 years?" Gabe and Pete voted to zoom forward so they could live in space. The 1814 option was more appealing to the rest of us.

An assent at mile 15 silenced Jim and I as we huffed and puffed our way to the top. My nephews kept an eye out for vultures circling the old meat. It was the pounding descent that silenced the young'ns; knees and legs throbbing. Gabe said it felt like his thighs had a heartbeat.

Like a mirage, the mission appeared in the distance. We reached it not a moment too soon. The little amount of energy left in our fuel tanks was used to tour Mission San Juan Bautista, the largest of all 21 religious landmarks. The main altar and six statues of the reredos was completed in the 1700s by a sailor who jumped ship in Monterey. He painstakingly painted the figurines in exchange for room and board.

The remainder of our day was spent dining on spectacular Basque food at a ma and pa restaurant near our hotel, and a rousting card game of gin rummy.

Mission #15: San Juan Bautista

Stories from the Slog...

LEG NINE, DAY THREE

Our Camino group gained a member, Bob Brunson, whose house we stayed at in Monterey. He is walking with us for two days. He's hiked a few sections of the Royal Road already, but not our weekend route from San Juan Bautista to the Santa Cruz Mission. Interesting thing about Bob – he's a Third Order Regular Franciscan. This means he patterns his life in the spirit of St. Francis of Assisi. These are generally laypersons who do not take religious vows but participate in the charitable works of the order. This also entitles him to wear a habit consisting of a brown hooded robe tied at the waist with a white rope. Three knots in his belt represent the vows of poverty, chastity, and obedience.

His piety is balanced by his witty sense of humor. Apparently, Franciscans are allowed to swear and drink. Bob's open-minded approach to spirituality endears everyone he meets. We all love his company. A huge smile comes upon his face as he greets strangers who stop, wanting to talk with him. Car horns honk and he waves. It's like walking with a celebrity :-).

The five of us started the day with mass at San Juan Bautista Mission. We were on the road by 8:30 a.m. Mother Nature treated us again with eucalyptus groves, wild blackberry bushes, and gentleman's farms along country roads. Driscoll's, the nations leading supplier of fresh berries, is headquartered in Watsonville, where we are overnighting. The last few miles of today's walk was among the fruit grower's fields.

We reached the American Value Inn about 5 p.m. ready to grab a shower and go eat. A carbo-loaded dinner at the local Mexican restaurant pushed us over the sleepy edge. Lights out by 9:30 p.m.

Never-agains from the Nephews...

LEG NINE, DAY FOUR

We were all circling the drain. Pete had an inflamed sciatic and bum left foot. Gabe was requesting a new pair of feet. Jim battled a blisterette. Friar Bob had the flu. And I wrestled with the usual heel and toe issues. Other than that, all was well :-).

Oatmeal, pancakes, eggs, and lots of coffee supplied the boost of energy we needed. The morning miles were along San Andreas Road, which hugs the fault line. Luckily the big one didn't hit. Within 7 miles the flu-inflicted Friar's fever proved too much. He was done! We knew he was feeling bad when we walked by the railroad tracks and he said "if a train comes, I'm either gonna jump on it or in front of it." His daughter fetched him at nearby Manresa Beach.

For the next 3 hours, we moseyed along the sands of the Pacific...Beer Can Beach, New Brighton Beach, China Beach. We looked a tad awkward dressed in full hiking regalia traipsing alongside scantily clad swimmers. I'm sure more than one person wondered what we were doing.

The hypothetical question of the day emerged as we headed north. "What President, dead or alive, would you like to have lunch with ?" Pete, Slick Willy. Jim, Lincoln. Gabe and me, Teddy Roosevelt.

We passed lots of RVs parked roadside enjoying the view and ocean air. Finally, at mile 18 we reached Capitola. Our original plan was to go the whole way to Santa Cruz Mission 5 miles further. NO WAY! The MST bus sounded much more appealing.

We arrived at the mission after it closed, but a wonderful docent unlocked the gates, showed us around, and took a group photo.

Our gang had walked 64 miles in four days...including 11-year old Gabe!

CHINA BEACH

DURING THE EARLY 1860's A SMALL VILLAGE CONSTRUCTED OF SCRAP LUMBER AND DRIFTWOOD WAS ERECTED AT THE BASE OF THESE CLIFFS. KNOWN AS CHINA BEACH, OR CHINA COVE, IT WAS ESTABLISHED BY CHINESE FISHERMEN WHO SET THEIR NETS BY BOAT AND THEN HAULED THEIR DAILY CATCH ONTO THE BEACH BY HAND FOR DRYING AND SELLING. BY 1880, HOWEVER, THE EXPANDING RESORT INDUSTRY AND WAVES OF ANTI-CHINESE SENTIMENT HAD COMBINED TO FORCE THE LAST OF THE CHINESE FISHERMEN OUT OF SANTA CRUZ COUNTY.

DEDICATED OCTOBER 20, 1984, BY THE MONTEREY VIEJO CHAPTER NO. 1846, E. CLAMPUS VITUS.

Captions from the Camino...

LEG TEN, DAY ONE

My buddy Marie Horn from San Diego is this month's newcomer. Jim and Friar Bob are joining us. The boys and I have become old pals by now, having traipsed hill and dale together for the past few months. Marie fits right in with her sense of humor. Ya can't walk the Camino without one.

Southwest Airlines chauffeured me from SoCal to San Jose. Marie arrived a few days earlier to spend time with her son who lives in the Bay Area. She met me at the airport and we caught a shuttle to Capitola, our starting point for the tenth leg of my mission walk. The remainder of our clan trickled in via car and train.

The next morning's departure felt like O-dark-30 when in reality it was closer to 8-light-30. We couldn't be expected to pass up the home made waffles, eggs, brewed coffee, et al included in our room price :-).

By 11:30 a.m. we reached the Santa Cruz Mission. You may remember, last month my nephews, Jim and I ended 5 miles short of the Santa Cruz Mission because our feet staged a coup and would no longer carry us. We hitched a bus ride to our final destination so the boys could see Padre Serra's old stomping grounds from the 1700s. The distance was recouped this month with habit -clad Brother Bob and Marie in tow.

In the mission courtyard stands a gargantuan redwood which looked like it touched the sky! Spectacular! It was our first spotting of the magnificent timbers rooted in Northern California. I hugged, Jim kissed, Marie and Bob posed with the beauty before heading out for Scott's Valley.

It was a short and simple hike to the small town, population about 11,500. Oddly enough, for such a dot on the map they sure have an excellent Japanese restaurant! And...it was a few short steps from our Best Western Inn. A curio cabinet in the Asian eatery's lobby holds "masus," wooden boxes to drink saki from. Regular customers sign their own box, using their same vessel each time they visit. Marie partook in Nagorie, a cold unfiltered sake. When she asked to take the box, the waiter answered with a smile, "you'll have drink a lot more than one." That's not conducive when walking 19 miles the next day. She left the masu behind without regret considering a 6:30 a.m. wake up call would be here before she knew it...

Mission #16: Santa Cruz

Fabulousness from the Forest...

LEG TEN, DAY TWO

One word describes today...BREATHTAKING! Mother Nature's magnum opus is displayed in NorCal's redwood forest. Our 19-mile walk took nine hours due to constantly craning our necks upward trying to absorb their immensity! The 2,000-foot ascent over the Santa Cruz mountains also added to our tardiness. But no one cared because we were enveloped in such a magnificent ecosystem.

Mountain Charlie Road was our thoroughfare most the way. Folklore states the area was named after a man of the same name who on May 8, 1874 was attacked by a Grizzly Bear which had sprung from the dense thicket. The beast grabbed Charlie, mauling his head and taking a 4" chunk from above his eye and nose. The town doc patched Charlie with a silver plate. It didn't stay on long and Charlie lived another 38 years disfigured by his wounds.

This story ties in interestingly with our walk. Marie introduced us all to the her favorite pastime – Geocaching. It's an outdoor activity of treasure hunting in which participants use a GPS to find containers (caches) full of goodies (swag) hidden globally by other Geocachers. One of the caches on our route was titled "Mtn. Charlie Bear Fight." We found it tucked among roadside rocks. And...it was a small bear statue! Apropos! Marie lead us from goodie to goodie via tips posted on the games website. Five in total. More are selected for tomorrow....

Summaries from the Sojourn...

LEG TEN, DAY THREE

The gentrified, affluent, and charming town of Los Gatos in Silicon Valley was today's starting point. Yesterday's redwoods were going to be hard to beat. But, we were pleasantly surprised with our morning jaunt through Vasona Lake Park.

Over 150 acres of bike paths, creeks, ponds, and wildlife make this Santa Cruz County's most popular recreational spot. In our rush to make the self imposed 8 a.m. departure time, Jim forgot his second set of hiking clothes in the hotel. He didn't realize it until we were too far away to turn back. Luckily, a phone call to the Los Gatos Inn remedied the problem and Jim's gear would be FedExed to his home.

It posed a bit of a problem while still on the road. When one carries four days worth of gear on their back, numerous changes of clothes are sacrificed in exchange for a lighter pack, making the ones you do have valuable. Jim's consolation was knowing none of us smelled good by day 3, so his stench wasn't noticeable. We reached Santa Clara Mission about halfway through our day's 16-mile walk. It is the only Mission located on a college campus, Santa Clara University, a private Catholic school where the mission was built in 1777. It's the oldest university in California. As with all the missions, it's beautiful. The huge cross at the front of the chapel is the original. It's been covered in redwood for durability. We spent an hour recharging our batteries by lounging on the mission lawn before heading the rest of the way to our hotel for the evening.

Mission #17: Santa Clara de Asis

Mishmash from the March...

LEG TEN, DAY FOUR

The gritty sidewalks of San Jose lead us to the final mission of this month's walk. Not every section can be beautiful, but the comradery sure made it fun. Jim was in "horse to the barn" pace, while Friar Bob, Marie, and I hung back and told stories from our lives. The heat wasn't too bad, but Bob's Friar habit on top of his shorts and tee was toasty at times. He threatened to go commando, but decided the chafing would be equally uncomfortable.

As we passed through the run-down neighborhoods, complete strangers stopped to greet Bob. A hug or handshake always accompanied by a few kind words from the Friar ensued. Their faces lit up as they went on their way. Bob truly is the real thing. Is he perfect? No. Does he proselytize? No. What he does do is embrace humans from all walks of life and religions. He doesn't judge, and sees himself as a servant.

As lunch time rolled around we found ourselves in an Asian community. Food choices were McDonalds or the cultural fare. Jim opted for the familiar, while the rest of us tried the Chinese chow. Yummm! Our dessert pastries looked like a piece of art. On our long, steady uphill to the Old Mission San Jose, Marie found a swag stuffed Geocache. My buddy let me take a gorgeous piece of Millefiori glass as a souvenir, and she replaced it with one of her signature trinkets. One mile later we arrived at our divine destination. Sixty-eight miles under our belts. For me, it's the 18th Mission I've reached.

Marie's son picked us up to stay at he, his wife, and dog's home in the wine country. A quick dinner and off to bed. I consider myself so lucky to have again shared this journey with good friends.

Mission #18: San José

Fun with Five Fab Females...

LEG ELEVEN, DAY ONE

Yesterday Southwest flight 198 whisked Peggy, Tami, Cindy, Karyl, and I from San Diego to San Jose to start the 11th leg of my mission walk. Everyone but Karyl are repeat offenders – or as they put it "suckers."

How quickly my co-walkers forget the magnitude of these monthly hikes. After Tami slogged scores of miles with me in February she told her co-workers "if I ever say I'm undertaking another segment with Maggie, wallop me on the shins with a crow bar to remind me of the pain." Apparently, a challenge usurps agony :-).

We started day one with a bang... 22.5 miles. Redwood City was our destination. Surprisingly, the namesake trees were few and far between, although the small town was charming. But I digress. By mid afternoon we reached the Dumbarton Bridge. One and a half miles in length, and 85 feet tall, the cement structure denotes the southern portion of the San Francisco Bay. Below is a national wildlife refuge, the largest on the west coast, covering 1,600 square miles. It's home to thousands of fish, birds, and other wildlife. Views from the top of the span were gorgeous. But, with 81,000 cars traversing the six lane bridge daily, we kept sightseeing to a minimum. A concrete barrier safeguarded us from oncoming traffic. After exiting the overpass we skirted the marchlands for another hour. Times like these I wish my iPhone was a Nikon.

We stumbled into the Holiday Inn Express at 7:30 p.m., ordered room service, watched The Amazing Race – which looked like amateur hour compared to what we'd just endured – and conked out.

The Lowdown from the Ladies...

LEG ELEVEN, DAY TWO

Day two and our herd has thinned. Tami shuffled the first two miles and called it quits. Her nemesis? Painful feet. We called a cab and off she went to our pitstop for the day, San Bruno Marriott. And, she took all our backpacks with her – a win win for everyone!

For the first time since this journey begun 740 miles ago, my fellow pilgrims and I walked the entire day directly on the El Camino Real (ECR). Traffic usually dictates a deviation off the Royal Road.

Strip malls, housing developments, and apartment buildings now stand where Junipero Serra forged the path over two centuries ago. Only the name remains the same. In our minds eye we tried to envision the trail unsullied by progress. Although, we all agreed Padre would've welcomed the grande frappuccinos along the route.

Because urban sprawl has encroached on Serra's mother road, plotting my course to circumnavigate the sections which are now freeway requires Google Maps and Ron Briery's ECR hiking guide. Three years ago the septuagenarian author walked the entire trail in 55 days straight, chronicling turn by turn directions. As if that isn't enough, Butch, as his friends call him, is presently re-hiking the Camino to find a shorter option. I'm not sure whether to commend him or commit him.

Anyway, lo and behold we ran into Ron in the afternoon! It was quite an honor to meet the man who penned the book that started mission enthusiasts modern day pilgrimages. We asked the Camino's Obi Wan Kenobi what's the secret to avoiding sore, blistered feet? He said "there is none, I just walk with the pain." Not the answer we wanted to hear. After a few blocks, Ron veered off to explore a path different than ours.

Sixteen miles after starting our day we arrived at the hotel to find Tami with her tootsies propped up,watching "Wedding Planner" on TV. While we strode the sidewalks, she took a dip in the pool, sunbathed, and napped. We'd be lying if we didn't admit a tinge of jealousy. We regaled her with our days adventures over dinner,
then off to bed.

Prattle from the Princesses...

LEG ELEVEN, DAY THREE

What we lacked in rural terrain yesterday, we made up for today. San Bruno Mountain State Park's 2,326 acres whooped us like a boot camp drill sergeant. What started as a benign little hill, abruptly skyrocketed to 1,315 feet, forcing us to clamber over scree while shouting expletives. Low-lying chaparral provided no relief from the scorching sun. Peggy scampered up the path like a mountain goat, Cindy requested a photo so she could show her husband what a bad a#% she is, and Karyl tried in vain to cool herself with a paper fan she brought in her backpack. Tami opted out for a second day and was back at the hotel fast asleep.

As expected, the views of San Francisco from the summit were outstanding! Worth every step of the climb. Without a doubt, The City by the Bay is an American jewel not to be missed!

We coasted down into the wonderful jumble of SF's 838,000 residents to the Mission San Francisco de Asis. Opened the year America became a nation, it's the city's oldest building. The surrounding Castro District, Noe Valley, and Upper Market Street neighborhoods worship together at the historic parish.

Due to our late arrival, we had to tour the mission quickly before it closed. No worries, because we had a prior dinner engagement. Lin and Vince Galea, California Mission Walker Facebook page members, had a Camino gathering comprised of those who've tackled either the CALmino (CA Camino) and/or the Camino de Santiago. Ten of us met at their 1911 Edwardian home and swapped stories over soup and salad. A lovely evening.

Mission #19: San Francisco de Asis

Contes from the Cadre...

LEG ELEVEN, DAY FOUR

One word describes the final day of this months trip...FANTASTIC!! It started with a walk across the Golden Gate Bridge! Exhilaration, marvel, child-like enthusiasm, and pure enjoyment filled us as we lingered taking photos and soaking up the experience. Our cameras couldn't capture the magnitude, so we amassed mental souvenirs. The towers were shroud in the customary fog, but sun shone on either end of the 1.7-mile structure which links San Francisco and Marin County.

The iconic span was an engineering feat when it opened in 1937. One of the architects, Irving Morrow, chose the orange color realizing it would complement the bay's cool gray and the blue skies. Combined weight of the towers, deck, anchorages, girders, and massive cables is 887,000 tons. My hand couldn't even get halfway around one of the suspension cables.

As much as we wanted to dawdle on this wonder of the modern world, we continued on to catch a ferry to Larkspur across the bay. Butch and Lin joined us at the boat to share in the comradery of our final few miles to the San Rafael Arcangel Mission. As we sped across the strait I thought Junipero Serra would have appreciated this high speed vessel over a dug out canoe .

We arrived at the Larkspur landing in half an hour. Our hardihood parade of seven hikers reached the mission within 45 minutes. The modest original adobe building stands beside the larger Saint Raphael Church which services the upscale high-tech enclave. As with all these missions, the beauty was visceral. And our different modes to arrive were a nice variance from the usual footpaths.

It's days like this when all the "why am I doing this?" are answered. When all the fatigue is worthwhile. When I feel so fortunate for such an opportunity.

Mission #20: San Rafael Arcángel

Winding Down the Wandering...

LEG TWELVE, DAY ONE

Today started the final leg of my 800-mile California mission journey. I saved this month's walk for my husband, Miguel, and I only. The two of us knocking out the last three day, 35-mile hurrah before crossing the finish line together.

For the past year Miguel's kept the home fires burning as I roamed The Royal Road. Honestly, I think he and the dog enjoyed having the house to themselves a few days every month :-). But he jumped at the opportunity to culminate my achievement with me. Okay, jumped may be a stretch. He acquiesced, knowing he couldn't put it off any longer.

With a smile on his face we boarded Virgin America to San Fran yesterday. Nice airline. Within 1 hour and 30 minutes we'd disembarked and were in the Super Shuttle to Marin County. After a good night sleep we arrived at San Rafael Mission about 7:30 a.m.

Even anticipating impending leg cramps and blisters, Miguel had pep in his step and was ready to experience the El Camino. Fall is in full throttle up here. Our path was lined with trees the color of fire and sun; bushes where bursting with crimson berries. A treat for those of us who live in Southern California.

The California Mission Walkers Facebook page pioneer, Steven Woody, lives in this area. Knowing we'd be here this week, he wanted to say hi. He caught up with Miguel and I for the last 30 minutes of today's walk. A joy to meet, as well as a wealth of mission knowledge. He's hiked to two of the landmarks, so far. Due to a thriving business, two young children, and a wife, his plate is too full now to walk the entire King's Highway. But it's on his bucket list. After seeing his zeal for the project I have no doubt he'll do it.

After meeting Steven, it dawned on me; throughout this sojourn my Camino mates have run the spectrum – my nephews whom I've know since their births, my husband who I met 24 years ago, friends new and old, and complete strangers I encountered on Facebook. How fortunate to have had the pleasure of sharing this experience with such and array of people. Each one enhancing my journey in their own way.

The Espinosa's Escapades...

LEG TWELVE, DAY TWO

It's always beneficial to get mission walk directions from a local. Steven, our Facebook friend we met yesterday, routed Miguel and I through his native 'hood on rural roads with less traffic and more wildlife. Our starting point was Olompali State Historic Park. The name comes from the Miwok Native American language and translates as "people." The tribes were indigenous to Northern California until the early 1850s. Within the first 30 feet on the trail, we spotted a rafter of wild turkeys grazing in a pasture. A young doe scampered across the path up ahead as we stared at our feathered friends. Loved it!

Early afternoon had us on a narrow country road reminiscent of Old MacDonald's Farm – with a moo moo here, and an oink, oink there – you get the picture. Some hoofed honeys were friendly enough to approach us, but not close enough to pet – just one affectionate pussy cat who wanted to play.

By 1:30 p.m. we reached Petaluma and ate lunch at the Wild Goat. Its house speciality was the four-legged tribe's sweet milky elixir whipped into creamy chèvre crusted with Moroccan spiced dried fruits and almonds, spread on lightly toasted crostini. Yummmmm. Took awhile to tear ourselves away from the restaurant to complete our final five miles for the day. With daylight saving time upon us, we had to reach our destination earlier, before dark.

Dusk was falling as we approached Adobe Road, our starting point for tomorrow. I called for a ride to our hotel via UBER. For months I heard about the on-demand car service which utilizes your smartphone and dispatch software to send the driver closest to you. I downloaded the app and requested an UBER X. Shortly afterwards Gerardo pulled up in his shinny clean Jeep. Ten dollars and fifteen minutes later we were delivered to the Sheraton. Cheaper than a cab and more fun. I'm hooked. Early to bed tonight so we can rise with the sun to start the very last day of my year long journey. A rewarding way to spend my 54th birthday.

Summary from the Sojourn...

LEG TWELVE, DAY THREE (FINAL DAY!)

Today, on my 54th birthday, at 12:30 p.m., Miguel and I reached the final mission of my year-long walk along the El Camino Real. For me it's been:

1,841,931 steps

796 miles

49 total days walking

21 Missions visited

25 different travel companions

2 tired feet

1 elated and grateful woman!

To sum up the entire experience without reflection would do the walk an injustice. So for now I'll just say wow, what a journey!

THE END OF THE MISSION TRAIL
1523 - 1823

MISSION
SAN FRANCISCO SOLANO

SONOMA STATE HISTORIC PARK

Mission #21: San Francisco Solano

Epilogue from the El Camino...

The following friends and family were instrumental in making this trip possible with hospitality, home-cooked meals, and camaraderie on the trail.

Tracey Elliott	Luis Espinosa	Marie Horn
Cindy Freeman	Dorinda McClure-Payne	Ron "Butch" Briery
Tami Dahl	Sheryl Collmer	Karyl Carmignani
Kurt and Rose Buckley	Genette Foster	Lin and Vince Galea
Curt Cragg	Bob and Teresa Brunson	Steven Woody
Jim and Sharon Lutz	Peter Reeves	
Roxanna Hayes	Gabe Espinosa	

and my husband...Miguel Espinosa

Thank you all so much.

San Francisco Solano (1823)
San Rafael Arcángel (1817)
San Francisco de Asís (1776)
SAN FRANCISCO
San José (1797)
Santa Clara de Asís (1777)
Santa Cruz (1791)
SANTA CRUZ
San Juan Bautista (1797)
San Carlos Borromeo de Carmelo (1770)
CARMEL

Nuestra Señora de la Soledad (1791)

San Antonio de Padua (1771)

San Miguel Arcángel (1797)

SAN LUIS OBISPO
San Luis Obispo de Tolosa (1772)

La Purísima Concepción (1787)
Santa Inés (1804)
Santa Bárbara (1786)
SANTA BARBARA
San Buenaventura (1782)

San Fernando Rey de España (1797)
San Gabriel Arcángel (1771)
LOS ANGELES

San Juan Capistrano (1776)

San Luis Rey de Francia (1798)

San Diego Alcalá (1769)
SAN DIEGO

3 2 1   FOUNDERS OF THE 21 MISSIONS
1. Fr. Junípero Serra, OFM
2. Fr. Fermín Lasuen, OFM
3. Other

Maggie Espinosa is an award-winning travel journalist and author whose coverage includes national and international publications, syndicated radio interviews, and reporting for ABC, NBC and CW TV. She authored The Privileged Pooch, Luxury Travel With Your Pet in Southern California, a 206-page guide profiling upscale pet-friendly hotels, restaurants, shops, and activities.

Espinosa has journeyed to five continents, and has lived in Europe and the Caribbean. In 2007 she summited 14,500 foot Mt. Whitney, followed by a Grand Canyon National Park rim-to-rim hike a few years later. Home is San Diego, California with her husband Miguel and pooch, Marcel.